Maine Lines

Maine Lines

Poems, serious and otherwise, about Maine

Harris Stewart

Illustrated by John C. Holden

Manufactured in the United States of America

Library of Congress Catalog Card Number: 98-60898

ISBN: 1-881539-21-0

Cover design: Pearl and Associates

Cover illustration: John C. Holden

Other books by Harris Stewart:

The 1960 Explorer Expedition

The Global Sea

Deep Challenge

El Desasfio Del Mar

The Id of the Squid

The H.M.S. Challenger Sketchbook

No Dinosaurs on the Ark

Grungy George and Sloppy Sally

Injections of Hospital Humor

Man Bites Doggerel

The Unpredictable Mistress

Dedication

To all who love the many facets of this jewel we call Maine, the real Mainers, the folks from away, the summer folk and the short-term tourists like the fall leaf-peepers, this small volume is dedicated.

Acknowledgments

Although most of these lines were composed over a number of years, the author expresses his gratitude to Capt. Craig Nelson of the NOAA ship *Malcom Baldrige,* (formerly the *Researcher)* for giving him two carefree weeks aboard as visiting scientist on the last leg of her final cruise (July-August 1996) during which the last of these poems were generated.

Special thanks go to Lt. J.G. Mark Halsbeck (NOAA Corps) from whom I blatantly plagiarized the idea behind "The Haddock's Tale" on page 35.

Finally, I thank my wife, Louise, who utilized her journalistic expertise to accomplish the fine-tuning that some of these verses required.

Introduction

For many, the State of Maine is a state of mind. Like any state, it has its good points and its bad. But in Maine, the many good ones far outweigh the few bad. This volume of poems includes examples of both, from our glorious fall foliage to our harsh winters, from our rocky headlands to our clean mountain lakes. There is a humorous side to Maine, so that is included, too. This then, is the real Maine, and we love it.

HARRIS STEWART
Scarborough, Maine

The Meaning of Maine

The State of Maine means a lot to me.
Her mountain lakes and shimmering sea,
Her forests where the pines grow tall
And the first crisp day of an early fall.
Fat seals sunning on an offshore ledge
And sanderlings skirting the water's edge.
The smell of smoke from wood fires burning
And the colors of fall when the leaves are turning
Fresh vegetables bought at a roadside stand
Are one of the gifts from our fertile land.
The distant flash of a lighthouse light
And a foghorn's moan on a foggy night.
We bundle up when it's cold and raw
In a scarf, woolly hat, bulky mackinaw.
When we're finished with winter's cold,
The coming of spring is a joy to behold.
All of these things you will have to see
To know what Maine really means to me.

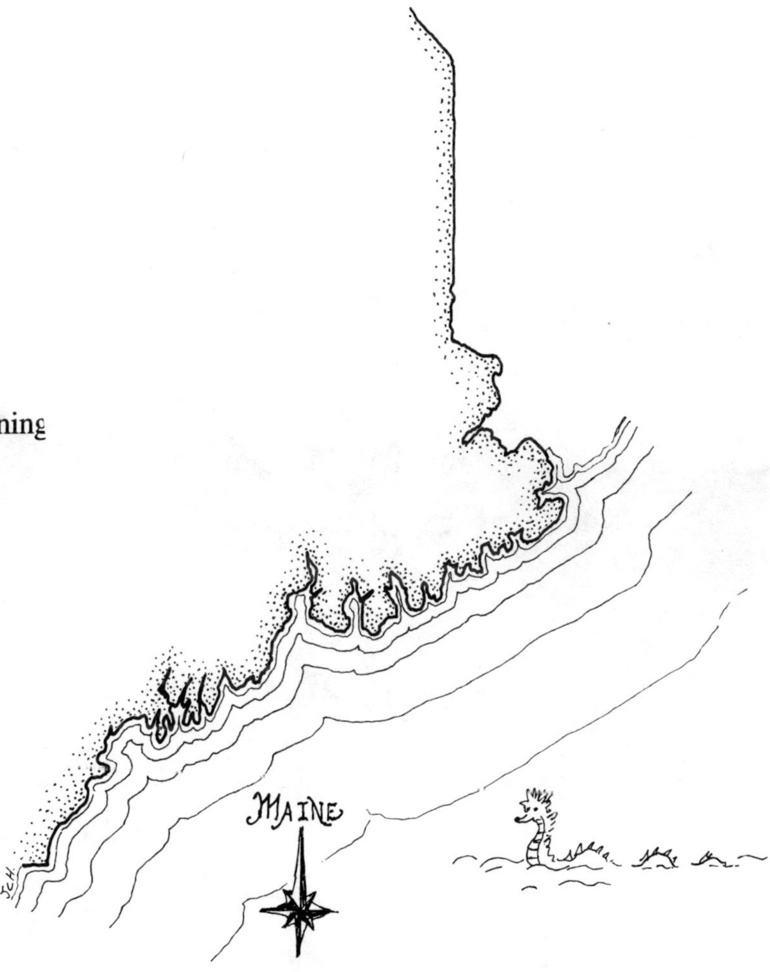

JCH

The Fisherman and Me

The bearded Down East fisherman
Who stopped me on my walk
Was a man I'd never seen before,
But he asked if we could talk.

So we looked and found a nearby bench
Where the man could look to sea,
And when he'd filled and lit his pipe,
He told this tale to me.

But first he asked how old I was.
At the time, I was just ten.
He was quiet for a moment,
Then he spoke to me again.

"Now, I quit school at your age, son,
So I could help my pa,
But lobster pots and fishin' nets
Was all I ever saw.

"I never learned much history,
And I still don't speak so good,
But I'm pretty good at carvin'
From most any chunk of wood.

"But there's more to life than carvin'
And tendin' pots and nets,
For it's what a feller knows
That determines what he gets.

"Now, I'm not knockin' fishin',
For the sea's been good to me,
But if I had more learnin'
There's more that I could be.

"So don't you do like I did,
Obey this simple rule:
Don't miss your chance at learnin'
By droppin' outta school."

Then the old man rose
And slowly walked away.
How could that man have known
That I'd quit school that day?

But I'd heard his message clearly,
And because I was no fool,
I somehow knew that man was right,
And I hurried back to school.

JCH

Maine Winters

I prayed that I would never see
Another winter like '93,
But Nature from her bag of tricks
Sent the horrible winter of '96.
For southern friends who want to know,
Here's how we coped with all that snow.
Main roads were clear because we'd planned
With heavy plows and salt and sand
To start the plowing when it's snowing
And continue while it's blowing.
I'm glad we had the larder stocked,
For snow soon had the doorway blocked.
The schools were closed, the stores were, too,
There's precious little we could do
Except to stay indoors and do
Those things that we'd been meaning to
For weeks on end while it was nice.
But now with all this snow and ice
We're trapped indoors with mundane tasks
'Til one of our young children asks,
"Who will come outdoors with me,
For I would really like to see
What the world is like all white,
It should be a lovely sight."
The boy was eager, so we put
On heavy clothes from head to foot,
Opened up the door a crack,
And slowly pushed the snowdrift back.
Once outside the boy was swift
To jump waist-deep into a drift.
Kids in snow do happy things
Like making snowy angel wings
By lying prone upon the snow
And moving outstretched arms just so,
Sometimes even grow-ups try it
While children's laughter breaks the quiet.
Otherwise, there's not a sound
When snow has blanketed the ground.
When spring has come, I'll know we've made it,
Though winter's fun, I'd gladly trade it
For warmer climes and southern friends
Until our northern winter ends.
Folks from away I thought insane
Who only summer here in Maine,
With '96 worse than '93,
I think the insane one is me.

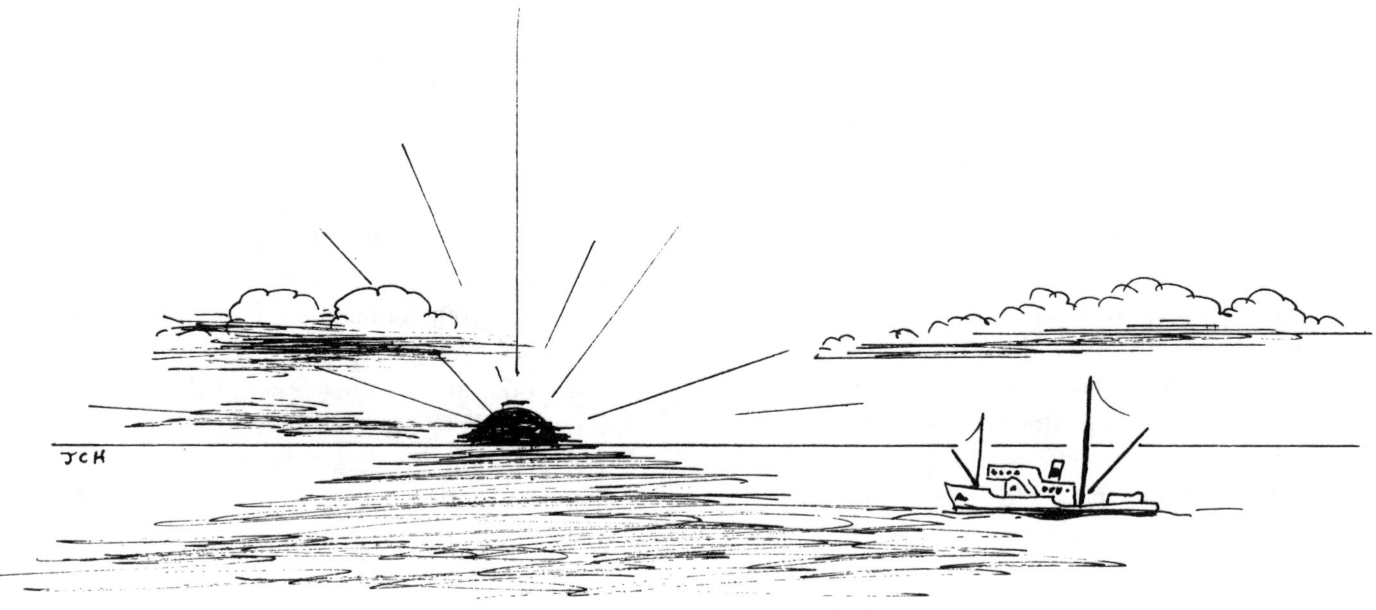
JCH

On Laying Up a Big Trawler

This trawler meant a lot to me,
Her gentle roll in a moderate sea,
The curtain swaying at her galley door
And a pencil rolling in an empty drawer.

The steady pounding of her study hull
And the raucous cry of a wheeling gull,
The sibilant sigh as a swell slid by
On a moonless night 'neath a starry sky.

Her ensign snapping in a spanking breeze
And flying foam from the wind-whipped seas,
The silent splendor of a rising sun,
And a few hours sleep when your watch was done.

Sorting the catch when the trawl came in,
Some days you lose, and some you win.
Unloading our catch, we'd go out again,
For the fishing was good in the Gulf of Maine.

The creaks and groans of this aging ship
Were friendly sounds on her final trip.
And those who have worked on a trawler at sea
Will know the joy of these things for me.

?
MAPLE
SYRUP
MADE IN
KOREA
JCH

A Plug for Our System

My watch was made in Taiwan,
My TV in Korea,
My car's made in Japan,
But we also make things heah.

We build good things in Maine
That you can't get from Asia
Like great wooden furniture
And crafts that will amaze ya.

So do your buying heah
Instead of overseas,
For Made in Maine means quality
And goods that always please.

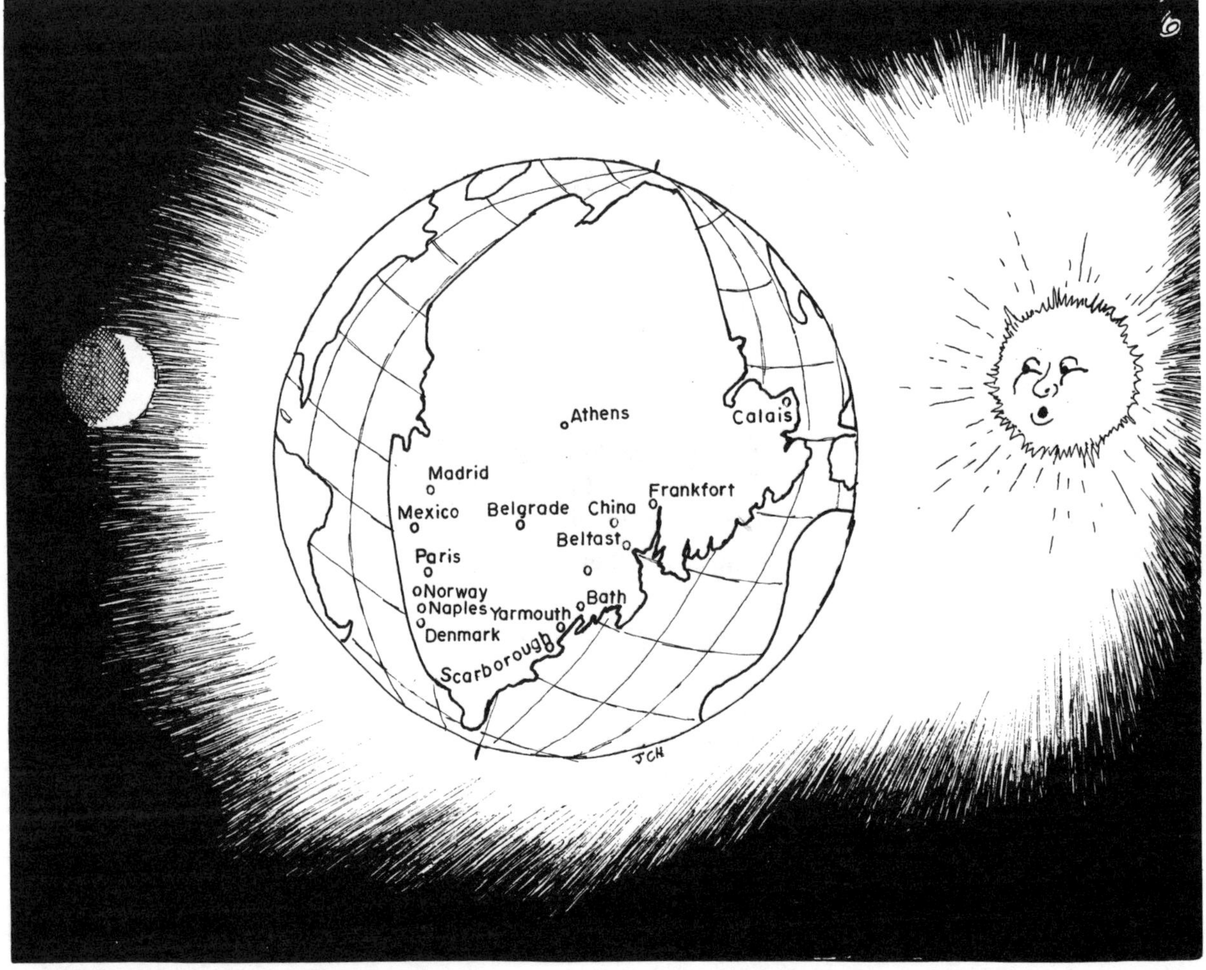
Athens
Calais
Madrid
Frankfort
Mexico
Belgrade
China
Beltast
Paris
Norway
Naples
Yarmouth
Bath
Denmark
Scarborough
JCH

Maine Town Names

There's China, Mexico, Denmark and Norway,
There's Athens, Bath, Madrid and Calais,*
Belfast and Belgrade to name just a few
And Moscow, Vienna and Frankfort, too.
You still wondering what to do?
Then visit Palermo and Naples, too.
More names from Britain than anyone needs,
There's Scarborough, Falmouth, Yarmouth and Leeds.
In my opinion, for what it's worth,
Town names in Maine are great,
For you can travel around the earth
Without ever leaving the state.

* Here we call it CALiss, but non-Mainers won't know that.

FREUD

A Fickle Herring from the Gulf of Maine

Now herring was a fish
Who did on one occasion
As lover take a whale,
She loved the big cetacean.

She always swam with whale
And spurned her fellow fishes.
And said, “Why shouldn’t I,
If that is what my wish is?”

When herring tired of whale
(She said the monster bored her),
She found a handsome seal
And lured the fellow toward her.

“And where is whale?” asked seal,
She squeezed her lover’s flipper.
“But why ask me?” said herring,
“Am I my blubber’s kipper?”

96
ME-123
HOLDEN

Moose

Look out for moose while driving,
For Maine is where they are.
Your car can hurt a moose,
But a moose can kill your car.

HOLDEN

We Have Twenty-foot Tides

When you tie up at a dock,
Check the tide before you go,
Or she'll be hanging by her painter
By the time the tide is low.

BOUX WOUX
NON NON!
CANADA
MAINE
CALAIS
ON WHICH SYL-AH́-BLE DO YOU PUT THE EM-PHEÉ-SIS?

Calais

Although some towns have foreign names,
We pronounce them without malice.
For example, it's not "caLAY,"
Instead, we call it "CALiss."

BUT CAN HE STILL
SMELL WHAT HE
TASTES ?
JCH

The Portland Pirates Hockey Team

Our poor hockey goalie
Has run out of luck.
He was hit in the teeth
By a hard-driven puck.
He said, "It's a hazard
Of the game I am playing,
With my eye teeth all gone,
I can't see what I'm saying."

(Tradition has it that Maine clams are the best when harvested September through April—the “R” months.)

A Cautionary Note

Unless your stomach is borrowed from Tarzan,
Limit your clamming to months that an R’s in.

SFA
AFRI
FRAN
JCH

She Loves the Food on the *Scotia Prince*

When her plate is full, she's glad
And stuffs 'til they remove it.
TRAVEL IS BROADENING, read the ad,
And she has hips to prove it.

JCH

The Haddock's Tale

I was a happy haddock
A-swimming in the sea,
Until one day I saw some bait
That really tempted me.

The morsel looked delicious,
And I thought perhaps I might
Swim a little closer
Just to take a little bite.

But it wasn't very tasty
In spite of how it looked.
I'm sorry that I tried it,
For I was firmly hooked.

They hauled me in and cleaned me,
So at least I wasn't wasted,
For they cooked me up for dinner,
And I wonder how I tasted.

HOLDEN

On the Beach

We spread out on our beaches,
But the high tide comes too soon.
So we all end up together
Jammed up against the dune.

WHAT DO YOU EXPECT FROM PEOPLE WHO WOULD SAY "CAL' iss"?
WELCOME TO
AINE
PORTSMOUTH NAVAL SHIPYARD
BOUX WOUX WOUX WOUX
JCH

Portsmouth Naval Shipyard

Portsmouth's in New Hampshire
And the shipyard gives them pain,
For the shipyard is in Kittery,
And the Kittery's in Maine.

L.L.BEAN
L.L. BEAN
JCH

The Tourists

The tourists love our scenery,
But it seems their favorite scene
Is the little town of Freeport
And the store of L.L. Bean.

My Garden

I have a little garden
And every day I pray
That someone invents something
To keep the deer away.

The Deer

Early in the fall
The deer are all around,
'Til hunting season opens
When none are to be found.

JCH

Maine Sports

All year long there's plenty to do.
We hike and we climb, we sail and canoe.
In the winter we skate, toboggan and ski,
But the water's too cold to swim in the sea.
Some Mainers swim when the weather is hot
They must be brave, but I'm glad that I'm not.

JCH

I-95 vs. U.S. One

I prefer traveling U.S. ONE,
For hugging the coast is a lot more fun
Than having to drive
On I-95
Where they go like a son-of-a-gun.

As our highways get wider and faster,
Speed is becoming our master.
I prefer to slow down,
Taking back roads to town,
Instead of courting disaster.

JCH

Folks from Away

Folks from away are welcome,
We're glad that they are here,
But most are quite reluctant
To stay throughout the year.

And when the leaves are turning,
More come by car and bus,
But we're glad when they are leaving,
To leave the state to us.

JCH

Migration

In the fall under azure skies,
We see migrating geese, monarch butterflies.
These creatures somehow know it's time
To head on south to a warmer clime.
And when our autumn color's through,
The summer folk will be migrating, too.

RULES
OF
GRAMMAR

It's a Great Store, but Pronounce It Right

I have trouble pronouncing S.S. Peirce,
But trying to spell it is even worse.
It's "I" before "E"
Except after "C"
Except in "neighbor" and S.S. Peirce.

OUI
OUI!
BOUX
WOUX!
FAUX
PAUX
JCH

Pierre and His Dog, Fido, Are Visiting from Quebec

He said, "It's one of several hounds.
Though it may seem strange to you,
I spell it just the way it sounds,
F.I.D.E.A.U."

JCH

Pocket Beaches

One of the sights of which we boast
Is our rockbound, stern and rugged coast.
But just be sure that you have seen 'em,
Those rocky headlands that have between 'em
Small pocket beaches we like the most.

At Scarborough Downs

Two trainers washing down a horse,
Each with a separate hose.
One man started at the tail,
The other at the nose.
When they met in the middle,
That could have swapped hoses, of course,
But they remembered the axiom
And didn't change streams in mid-horse.

JCH

Rescue Mission

Maine has a maritime heritage
Going back for many a year,
For we fed the Pilgrims at Plymouth
By shipping potatoes from here.

JCH-AIR

Mostly Small Planes in Maine

I will not fly on those big jets,
But fly small planes because
A crash kills fewer people
Than when a big jet does.

JCH

The Good Life in Maine

Most of us real Mainers
Live along the coast,
For the fishing and the sailing
Are the things we like the most.
But we also like the mountains,
So when we get a break
We retire to the cabin
That we built beside a lake.

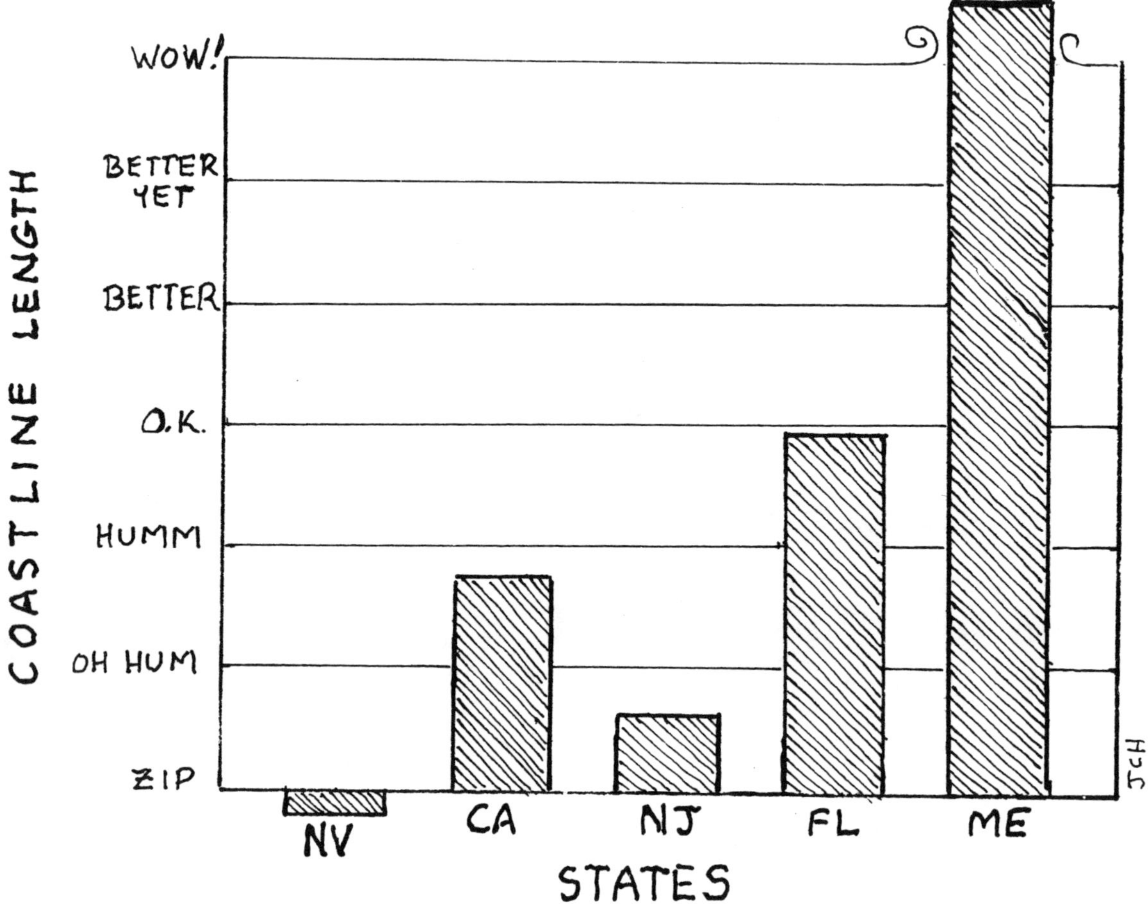
WOW!
BETTER YET
BETTER
O.K.
HUMM
OH HUM
ZIP
COASTLINE LENGTH
NV
CA
NJ
FL
ME
STATES
JCH

It's Long and Beautiful

Including the bays and islands
In the coastline of our state,
Gives Maine the longest coastline
Of all the forty-eight.

JCH

Minor, My Foot!

With only one minor exception,
Baxter State Park is a winner,
But late in the day the deer flies come out
With the thought that I am their dinner.

JCH

A Comment from Maine's Most Remote County

"The livin' here ain't easy,
It's full of toil and strife,
But few of us would leave it,
For it's a happy life."

Come and $tay for Awhile

You'll find our state is beautiful,
The best you've every seen,
So come and bring your money,
It helps to keep Maine green.

EXXIT
REGULAR
$3.69 9
I'M JACK
TRUST ME
EXXIT
GAS
"PUT A TANKER ON YOUR TIGER"
FLORIDA 97
IC STEW
SSSSSSS
JCH

Taxes

Summer folks aren't residents,
They're here for too few days.
Sure, they pay no income tax,
But we get them other ways.

JCH

Why Not?

Wiping out our forests
Would seem to be the plan,
For we ship out all those logs
Across the ocean to Japan.

There they take our timber
And with very little fuss
Turn it into plywood
And sell it back to us.

There's got to be a better way,
To me a plan is clear.
We build ourselves a plant in Maine
And make the plywood here.

JCH

The Lobster

That first man was very brave
And none can ever beat it
Who pulled a lobster from the sea
And said, "I'm going to eat it."

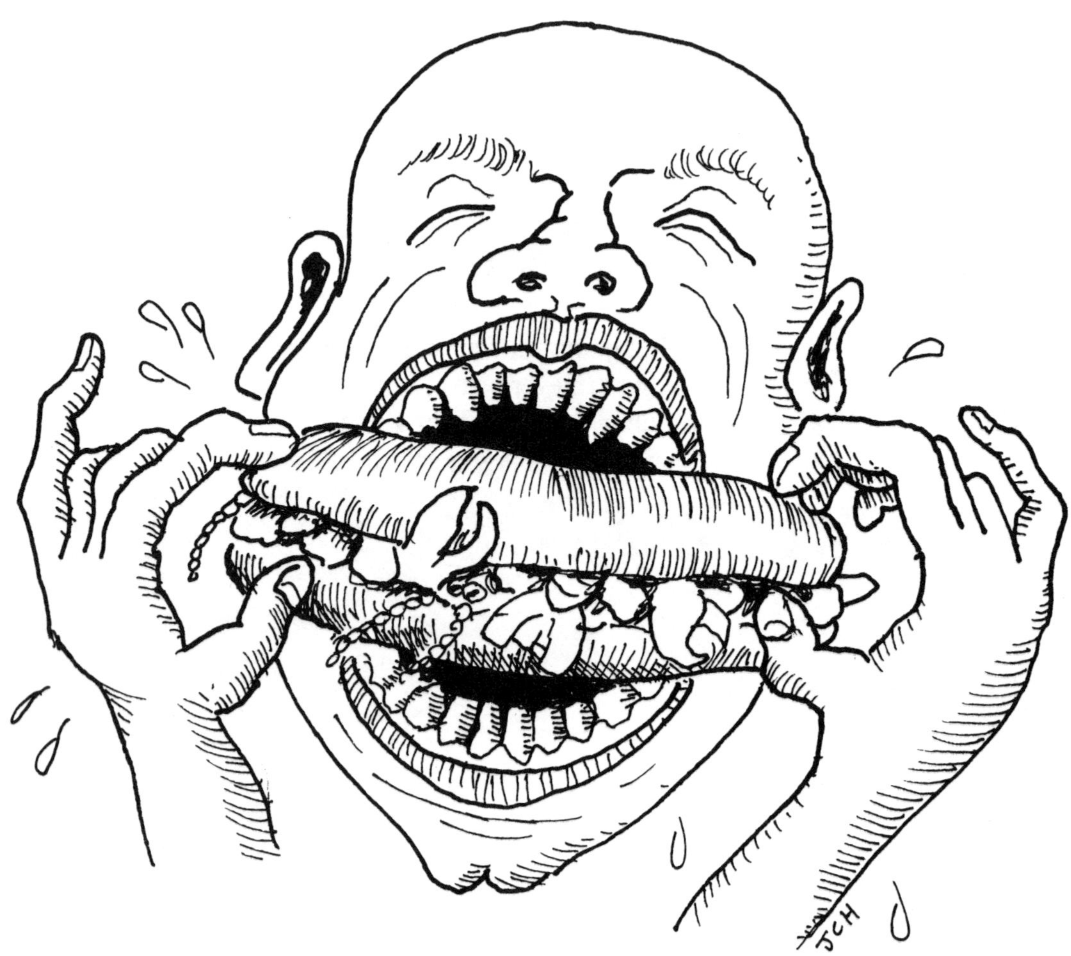
JCH

The Good Maine Lunch

My favorite lunch and a noontime goal
Is a good clam chowder and a lobster roll.

JCH

We Have Culture, Too

Our museums are good, be sure to see 'em.
The best? The Penobscot Marine Museum.
Each year the ballet and concerts start,
And there's always the Portland Museum of Art.
There's the Farnsworth and galleries galore,
And Homer's studio beside the shore.
All year long we find plenty to do,
If you lived here, then you would too.

?!!
JCH

Stew's Law

From my many years of sailing,
There's one thing I have found:
When your draft exceeds your water depth,
You surely are aground.

JCH

The Great Ice Storm of '98

We survived that awful storm,
For we've got what it takes,
And we needed that ice storm
Like a turtle needs air brakes.

After Spending the Winter of '96 in Rockport

I dislike making platitudes,
But I like warmer latitudes.

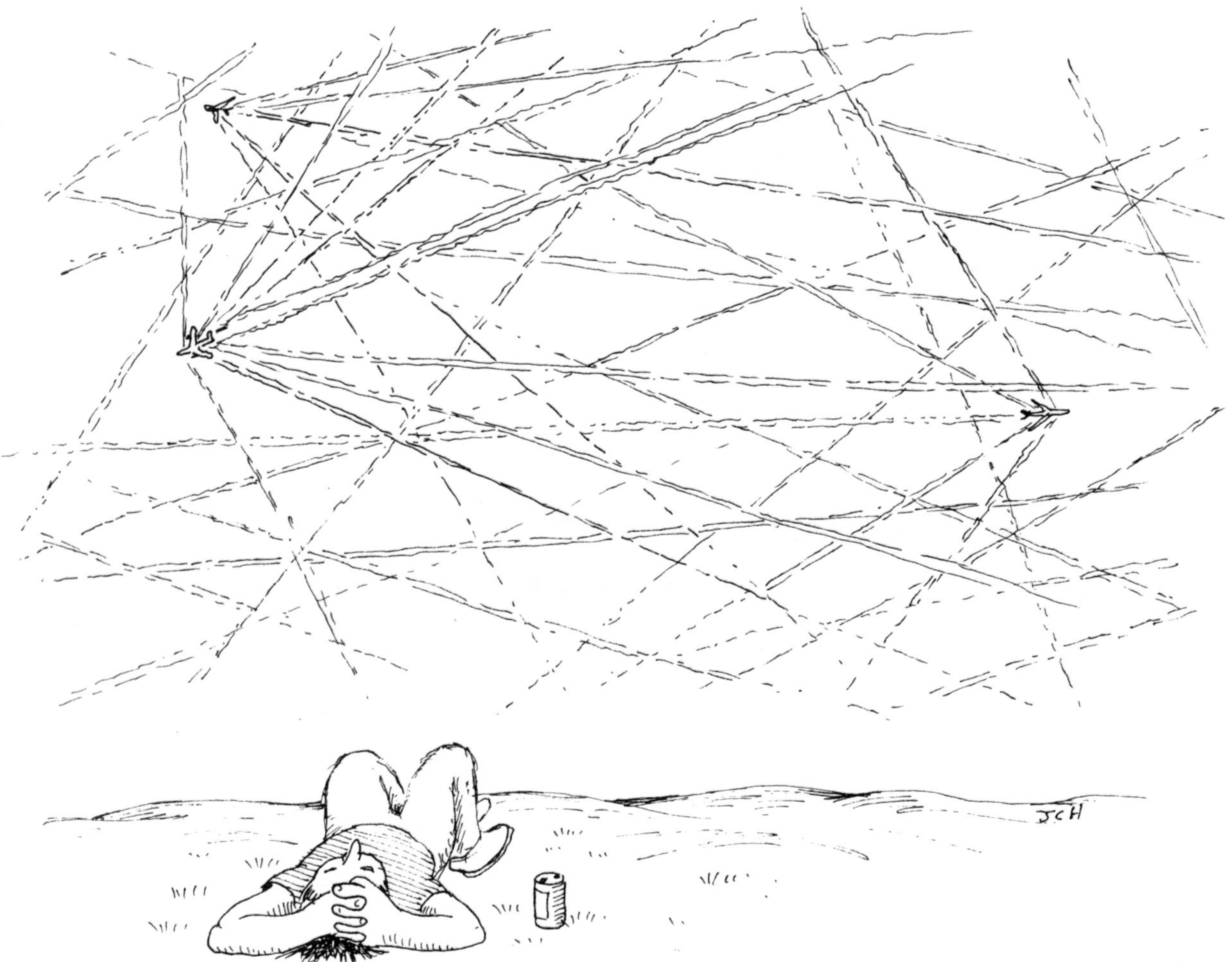
JCH

Thank Goodness!

Those jets that fly so very high
Leave long white scratches on our sky.
And those power boats that flee
Leave long white streaks upon our sea.
We're most thankful they soon fade,
For what a mess if they all stayed.

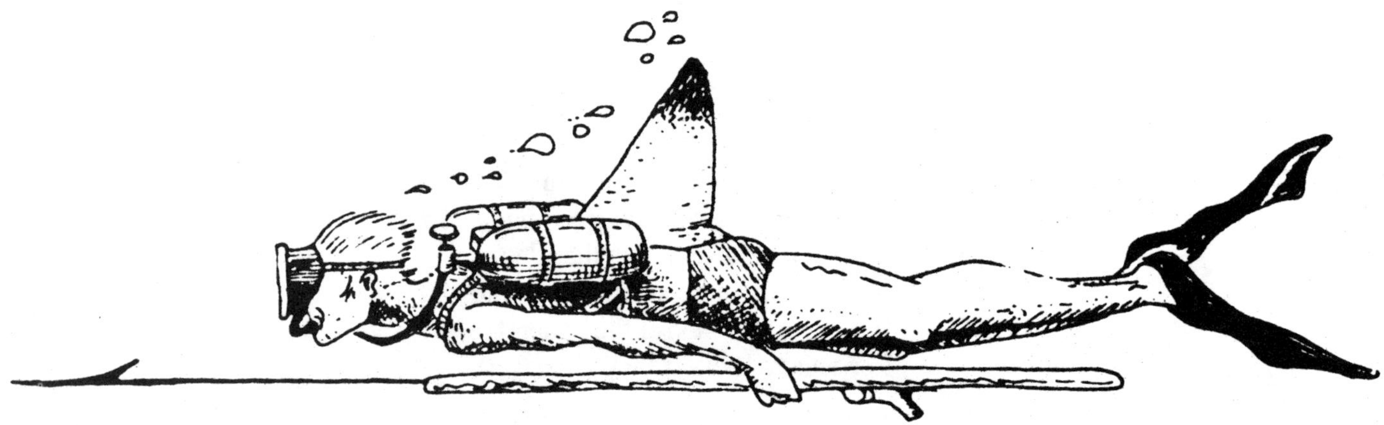

Moreso Than Sharks

Our ocean creature that we most fear
Is the SCUBA diver who carries a spear.

JCH

SCUBA

We never SCUBA dive alone,
And always dive with care,
For just outside the breakerzone, a steep drop-off is there.

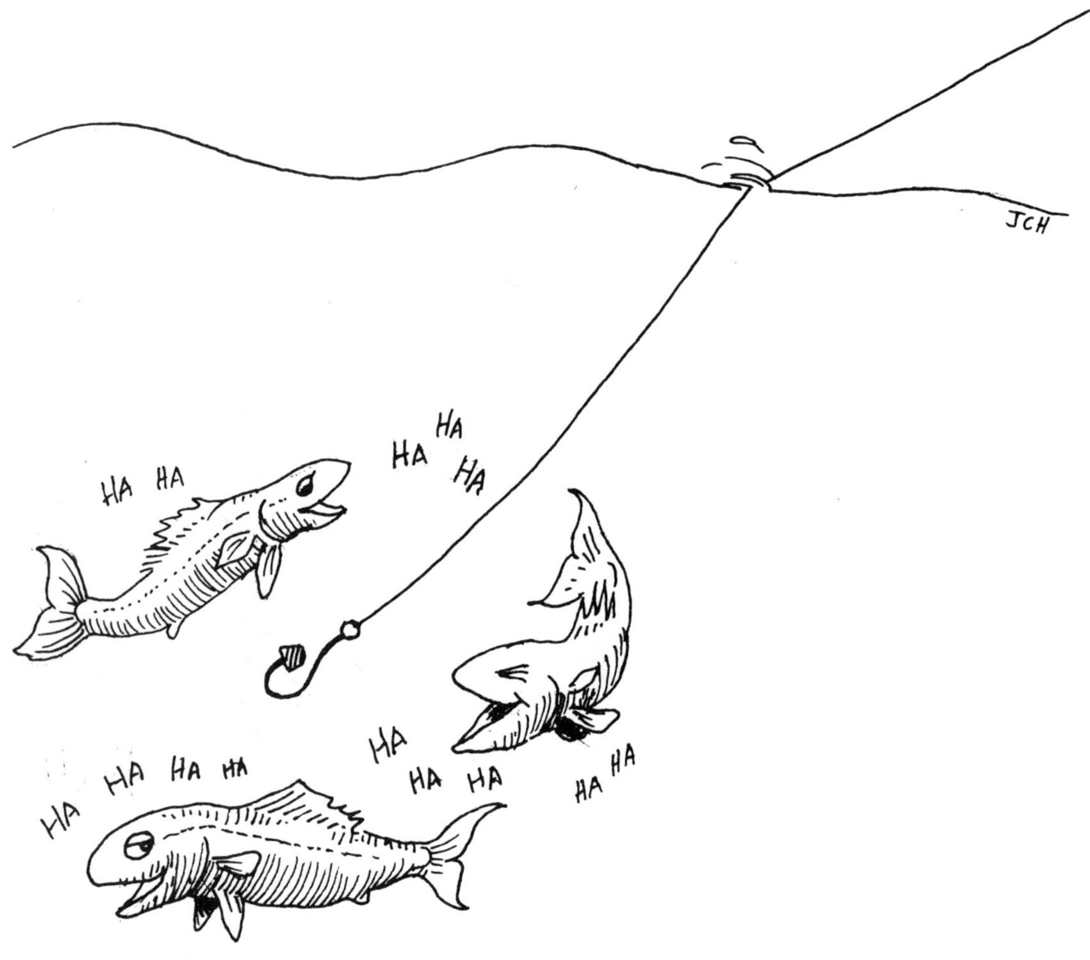
JCH
HA HA
HA
HA
HA
HA
HA HA HA HA
HA
HA HA
HA HA

The Happy Fisherman

I saw a happy fisherman
Out there upon the rocks.
But I could see from where I was
No fish were in his box.

So I shouted, "How's the fishin'?"
And he called from where he stood,
"The fishin' is terrific,
But the catchin' ain't so good."

Her Husband Has a 36-Foot Sailboat

She no longer joins him cruising,
"Because," she says, "I found
It's living in a prison cell
With a chance of being drowned."

JCH
JULY
1997
S M T W T F S
SPRING 1 2 3 4 5
6 7 8 9 10 11 12
SUMMER
13 14 15 16 17 18 19
20 21 22 23 24 25 26
27 28 29 30 31 FALL
!
SUMMER WAS MID JULY THIS YEAR!!!
? ?

Maine Summers Can Be Short

Spring was late and fall came early,
It will happen again, I fear.
Our summer didn't last for long,
It came on a Tuesday this year.

MAIL

Summer Aftermath

Our daughter from her summer friend
Received an autumn billet-doux,
While our mail at summer's end
Is filled with billies overdue.

Sea Monsters in Maine?

Over many years in Maine
I've heard some people say
They've spotted big sea monsters
In South Penobscot Bay.

So I gathered all the data,
All the witnesses' reports,
How they think the monster looks,
How the ugly beast cavorts.

With the size (from thousand-footers
Down to little teeny weenies)
I've found good correlation
With the number of martinis.

News item: Diving physiologists are preparing a special questionnaire for divers in an effort to determine the extent of the after effects of prolonged SCUBA diving in Maine's cold waters.

Question One

Do you find that your diving
Detracts from your wiving?

NOT YET!
FRENCH - ENGLISH DICTIONARY
JCH

That's Maine Fer Ya!

I met a man in Lubec,
As Down-Maine as they get.
"Have you lived here all your life?" I asked,
And he replied, "Naut yayet."

About the Author

Harris Stewart, born in Auburn, New York, is a graduate of Exeter and Princeton, and holds a Ph.D. degree in oceanography. He was an Army Air Corps pilot in the Southwest Pacific during World War II and retired as a government scientist in 1978.

Although in this small volumne he sounds like a native Mainer, he reluctantly admits to being one of the folks from away of whom he pokes fun. He has ten published books, five of humorous light verse.

He and his wife, Louise, spend as few winter months as necessary in Naples, Florida, before returning to Scarborough on the Maine coast for the summer.

And the Illustrator

John Holden has a bachelor's and master's degrees from San Diego State College. An avid cartoonist, he has a long career as a scientific illustrator and has illustrated several books, including four by Harris Stewart. He now lives in the foothills of the Cascade Range in Washington State, where he taught geology and astronomy until his retirement in 1997.